A Choice of Shelley's Verse

A CHOICE OF SHELLEY'S VERSE

*Selected with
an introduction by
Stephen Spender*

faber and faber

LONDON BOSTON

First published in 1971
by Faber and Faber Limited
3 Queen Square London WC1
Reprinted 1973, 1977, 1984 and 1988
Printed in Great Britain by
Richard Clay Ltd, Bungay, Suffolk
All rights reserved

ISBN 0 571 08790 6

Contents

[5]

Introduction

If we hear the name 'Shelley' we do not know whether to think of the man or of the poetry. More than with other poets, the two seem interfused.

Shelley belonged to the second phase of romanticism, after Wordsworth and Coleridge, when the subjectivity which Keats called the 'egotistical sublime' in Wordsworth, and which characterized romantic poetry, seems to have entered a new phase: the poet becomes the poetry, the poetry the poet. The lives of Byron, Keats and Shelley all seem poems written by themselves: and when we judge their poetry we feel we are not judging some external artefact, the poem, but the poets.

'Oh for a life of pure sensation,' wrote Keats: by which he meant that he longed for a life of experiences identical with those of poetry, become as it were, the sensuous body which he could inhabit. And Shelley lived his life as Godwinian philosopher, spiritual lover, out of the same imagination as he lived and wrote his poetry: an imagination revolutionizing society, moving into human affairs, public and private, and which might control—when men came to 'imagine that which we know'—even science and political economy. Hence the poets as the 'unacknowledged legislators'. The poet has taken the world upon himself as a problem of the unimagined which he seeks to solve by the imagination. But the world which refuses to respond to such a transformation of concrete things into spiritual dreams and ideas, crucifies him, just as Christ, whom Shelley did not believe in, was crucified by man's refusal to see all things under the aspect of divine love.

When the outer world refused to conform to the poetic vision the poet experienced a disappointment which, quite literally, killed him.

Of the three romantics—Byron, Keats and Shelley—who met early deaths, Shelley is the one who has drawn most upon himself and his poetry the disparagement attaching to a personality with qualities inescapable and unacceptable. In several of his poems he is a presence felt, making claims on our attention and sympathy which we cannot accommodate, and which sometimes repel. We cannot tolerate the hysterical shriek: 'I bleed upon the thorns of life!/My heart breaks loud and fast/Oh press it to thine own again/where it will break at last.'

'Alas, poor Shelley!' exclaimed Keats. And his drowned corpse comes back to us hung round with the trophies of his personal legend, like a figure out of Dante's Purgatorio: hated squire father Sir Timothy, adored sisters, poor drowned Harriet, treacherous James Jefferson Hogg, world-changing, idealistic, impecunious father-in-law Godwin, and all those Janes, Harriets, Claire Clairmonts, etc.: the whole put together, edited, examined, explained by severe Mary Shelley, surviving among Victorians, writing novel after novel across which Shelley's ghost flitted, whilst his shrivelled heart, enclosed in an envelope and given her by Trelawny, lay pigeon-holed on her desk, burning with inspiration and ashen with regrets.

Inevitably the modern reader sympathetic to Shelley approaches his *Collected Poems* with trepidation. One fears for him: that he will be too self-righteously opinionated, too miserably self-pitying, too transcendentally passionate—brother body-soul melting into sister body-soul.

He remains controversial not merely for this presence of

a biographical *persona* in so much of his work, but for his strained metaphors, unidentifiable imagery. Eliot, in the late twenties, led the assault by comparing the imprecise metaphors of the lines beginning 'Light of life thy lips enkindle' unfavourably with Dryden, and raising the awkward question—what star or planet is referred to in the lines (from *To A Skylark*):

> Keen as are the arrows
> Of that silver sphere,
> Whose intense lamp narrows
> In the white dawn clear
> Until we hardly see—we feel that it is there.

Surely it is the moon. But readers certainly disagree about this, which goes to show that Eliot's charge of vagueness has force. Perhaps though one can suggest that Shelley's indefiniteness in his references to external nature is the result of his intense subjectivity. Nature is always in process of becoming his own inner mood in his poetry and the distinctions between subjective and objective worlds become blurred. The force of the impression produced by the narrowing of 'the intense lamp' is achieved in the last line 'Until we hardly see—we feel that it is there'. One might ask whether if we hardly see but only feel the presence of the luminous sphere, do we have to identify it?

Later, Eliot attacked Shelley for the moral view expressed in his famous lines (printed here) about marriage—or some marriages—in *Epipsychidion*. This passage, however, has its defenders; and Forster's novel *The Longest Journey* is partly a gloss on the theme of those who

> With one chained friend, perhaps a jealous foe,
> The dreariest and the longest journey go.

No one—not even Browning and Meredith—has ever

been completely happy with Shelley's poetry. Yet Shelleyans are strangely persistent. They include Thomas Hardy and W. B. Yeats. Shelley is indeed like a phantom which disappears and yet haunts. There is surely no better example of this than Matthew Arnold's famous metaphor dismissing the ineffectual angel beating its luminous wings in vain: an image more haunting than any in Matthew Arnold's poetry. By way of Arnold a Shelleyan ghost shines through Eliot's lines in *Ash Wednesday*:

> Because these wings are no longer wings to fly
> But merely vans to beat the air.

Eliot came to regard *The Triumph of Life* (particularly the passage about Rousseau which I have included here) as the most Dantesque poetry in the English language. And he recognized Shelley's unique force in conveying a mystical sense of the meaning of life on earth when he made his character Reilly in *The Cocktail Party* quote the lines about the Magus Zoroaster from *Prometheus Unbound*:

> Ere Babylon was dust,
> The Magus Zoroaster, my dead child,
> Met his own image walking in the garden.
> That apparition, sole of men, he saw.
> For know there are two worlds of life and death:
> One that which thou beholdest; but the other
> Is underneath the grave, where do inhabit
> The shadows of all forms that think and live
> Till death unite them and they part no more;

The same passage and the lines which follow it, worked powerfully on Yeats's imagination throughout the whole of his life, which they span. For the young Yeats of the Dublin Hermetic Society declared that the dreams and imaginings of men of genius existed as realities in the universe, which was itself a dream. The same speech continues:

Dreams and the light imaginings of men,
And all that faith creates or love desires,
Terrible, strange, sublime and beauteous shapes.
There thou art, and dost hang, a writhing shade,
'Mid whirlwind-peopled mountains; all the gods
Are there, and all the powers of nameless worlds,
Vast, sceptred phantoms; heroes, men, and beasts;
And Demogorgon, a tremendous gloom;
And he, the supreme Tyrant, on his throne
Of burning gold. . .
                                   Call at will
Thine own ghost, or the ghost of Jupiter,
Hades or Typhon, or what mightier Gods
From all-prolific Evil, since thy ruin
Have sprung, and trampled on my prostrate sons.
Ask, and they must reply. . .

  Implicit here are Yeats's antimonies, like calling to
like, and also to its opposite. 'Call at will thine own
ghost, or the ghost of Jupiter,' Prometheus calling to his
opposite, and the object of his hatred, is echoed in:

Before me floats an image, man or shade,
Shade more than man, more image than a shade;
For Hades' bobbin bound in mummy-cloth
May unwind the winding path;
A mouth that has no moisture and no breath
Breathless mouths may summon;
I hail the superhuman;
I call it death-in-life and life-in-death.

  Prometheus Unbound, Hellas and *The Triumph of Life*, take
us a long way from the Shelley of *Queen Mab* and *The
Revolt of Islam*: though the Platonist Shelley, Berkleyan
rather than Lockian or Godwinian, with his strong pro-
pensity to regard the conflicts of this world as the reflec-

tion of conflicts between spiritual forces of which our reality is only the symbol, and to think of the flesh as a veil to be torn aside in a relationship which becomes an ideal spiritual union, was present from the first. There are indeed in Shelley's nature very striking opposites, the most obvious of which, in his life, are the disguised egoism (for which Harriet suffered so much) and the remarkable disinterested detachment which enabled him to treat his father-in-law Godwin with such patience and calm generosity. And in the poetry there is the subjectivity which I have mentioned which is too easily projected into revolutionary views for which modern psychology can find simple explanations: but there is also something quite different, an impersonality and objectivity of tone comparable with Goethe (Shelley translated the *Prologue in Heaven*, from *Faust*). This side of Shelley is sufficiently developed for me to suggest that if he had lived his poetic development might have been parallel with that of Goethe, who changed from the extreme, sometimes hysterical subjectivity of his earlier *Sturm und Drang* period, to the classical objectivity of his later work.

Like Goethe, Shelley had sensibility and intellect capable of absorbing a great deal of theory, information, and philosophy, and transforming them into his imaginative language. It is when he does this that he leaves the self-pitying lover and the ardent rebel furthest behind and enters a stratosphere of ideas into which is absorbed Greek philosophy, oriental mysticism, *The Divine Comedy*, *Faust*, and a good deal of miscellaneous historic and scientific information.

Deeper than the opinions and the neuroticism, there moves in Shelley that which Goethe anticipated from poetry: a world imagination, in which all pasts as well as the present, the landscapes of the several continents and their civilizations, are contained. For density of digested and transformed information communicated in a succession of shifting images, *Prometheus Unbound* compares only with *Faust* (particularly the second part of that poem). And when Shelley combines his most happily personal with his most objective qualities, in *The Invitation* one can agree that Baudelaire was not deceived in being influenced by this poem. And only Rimbaud in *Bateau Ivre* embarked on a voyage as fantastic as *Alastor*.

Shelley frequently has images of objects or persons dissolving in the intensity of their own radiance, and this may serve as a metaphor of what sometimes happens in his own poetry. Perhaps also the faintings and swoonings —results of a too spiritualized physical being?—which occur so often in his work, and which so repelled D. H. Lawrence, express the collapse of language in the presence of too luminous a vision.

It is understandable then that despite his having been so widely dismissed by modern criticism, Shelley remains a disturbing poetic presence, even among modern poets who cannot accept his personality or his style. It may be said, I think, that his imagination is greater than the forms he uses and that his language, though nearly always extraordinary and sometimes magnificent, manages often to be inadequate at the same time. Words and images fly off his impetuous stream of thought like fragments shattered by it, so that it is possible to think of the imagination as being separate from words and forms used, just as one can sometimes think of the idea in a work of Beethoven as being greater than the music.

I have put Shelley's fragment about the mind—incoherent though it is—at the front of this selection to show how Platonic was his idea of the intellect. The mind draws up knowledge and memories, instincts and feelings from human depths, and illuminates them.

In selecting poems, I have tried to keep Shelley's personal qualities as well as his poetic character in view. I have occasionally made cuts, which may be irritating to some readers, and I have drawn on fragments from the poet's notebooks which, although not always important as poetry, provide dazzling insights into the working of his imagination.

To print only the last three stanzas of the *Hymn to Intellectual Beauty* requires excuse. But the first four stanzas seem to me Wordsworthian without being as good as the best Wordsworth, whereas the last three are revealing autobiographical confession.

It may seem inexcusable to some readers that I have omitted *Adonais*. I do so firstly because it is so well known that I thought I might use the space it would occupy in a small selection by choosing less familiar examples. Secondly, I have another reason, which is that I think it the most Miltonic and least spontaneous of Shelley's more ambitious productions. Of course there is the marvellous ending containing the most lucid, radiant and eloquent expression of Shelley's platonism. To excerpt this may seem vulgar, but it does provide a fitting conclusion to this introduction:

LII

The One remains, the many change and pass;
  Heaven's light forever shines, Earth's shadows fly;
Life, like a dome of many-coloured glass,
  Stains the white radiance of Eternity,
  Until Death tramples it to fragments.—Die,
If thou wouldst be with that which thou dost seek!
  Follow where all is fled!—Rome's azure sky,
  Flowers, ruins, statues, music, words, are weak
The glory they transfuse with fitting truth to speak.

LIII

Why linger, why turn back, why shrink, my Heart?
Thy hopes are gone before: from all things here
They have departed; thou shouldst now depart!
A light is passed from the revolving year,
And man, and woman; and what still is dear
Attracts to crush, repels to make thee wither.
The soft sky smiles,—the low wind whispers near:
'Tis Adonais calls! oh, hasten thither,
No more let Life divide what Death can join together.

LIV

That Light whose smile kindles the Universe,
That Beauty in which all things work and move,
That Benediction which the eclipsing Curse
Of birth can quench not, that sustaining Love
Which through the web of being blindly wove
By man and beast and earth and air and sea,
Burns bright or dim, as each are mirrors of
The fire for which all thirst; now beams on me,
Consuming the last clouds of cold mortality.

LV

The breath whose might I have invoked in song
Descends on me; my spirit's bark is driven,
Far from the shore, far from the trembling throng
Whose sails were never to the tempest given;
The massy earth and spherèd skies are riven!
I am borne darkly, fearfully, afar;
Whilst, burning through the inmost veil of Heaven,
The soul of Adonais, like a star,
Beacons from the abode where the Eternal are.

Fragment: To the Mind of Man

Thou living light that in thy rainbow hues
  Clothest this naked world; and over Sea
   And Earth and air, and all the shapes that be
    In peopled darkness of this wondrous world
The Spirit of thy glory dost diffuse
      truth   thou Vital Flame
  Mysterious thought that in this mortal frame
Of things, with unextinguished lustre burnest
    Now pale and faint now high to Heaven upcurled
That eer as thou dost languish still returnest
  And ever
Before the   before the Pyramids
  So soon as from the Earth formless and rude
  One living step had chased drear Solitude
Thou wert, Thought; thy brightness charmed the lids
  Of the vast snake Eternity, who kept
  The tree of good and evil.—

FROM *Hymn to Intellectual Beauty*

V

While yet a boy I sought for ghosts, and sped
  Through many a listening chamber, cave and ruin,
  And starlight wood, with fearful steps pursuing

Hopes of high talk with the departed dead.
I called on poisonous names with which our youth is fed;
   I was not heard—I saw them not—
   When musing deeply on the lot
Of life, at that sweet time when winds are wooing
   All vital things that wake to bring
   News of birds and blossoming,—
   Sudden, thy shadow fell on me;
I shrieked, and clasped my hands in ecstasy!

VI

I vowed that I would dedicate my powers
   To thee and thine—have I not kept the vow?
   With beating heart and streaming eyes, even now
I call the phantoms of a thousand hours
Each from his voiceless grave: they have in visioned bowers
   Of studious zeal or love's delight
   Outwatched with me the envious night—
They know that never joy illumed my brow
   Unlinked with hope that thou wouldst free
   This world from its dark slavery,
   That thou—O awful LOVELINESS,
Wouldst give whate'er these words cannot express.

VII

The day becomes more solemn and serene
   When noon is past—there is a harmony
   In autumn, and a lustre in its sky,
Which through the summer is not heard or seen,
As if it could not be, as if it had not been!
   Thus let thy power, which like the truth
   Of nature on my passive youth
Descended, to my onward life supply
   Its calm—to one who worships thee,
   And every form containing thee,

Whom, SPIRIT fair, thy spells did bind
To fear himself, and love all human kind.

Dedication to *The Revolt of Islam*

> There is no danger to a man, that knows
> What life and death is: there's not any law
> Exceeds his knowledge; neither is it lawful
> That he should stoop to any other law.—CHAPMAN.

TO MARY —— ——

I

So now my summer task is ended, Mary,
  And I return to thee, mine own heart's home;
As to his Queen some victor Knight of Faëry,
  Earning bright spoils for her enchanted dome;
  Nor thou disdain, that ere my fame become
A star among the stars of mortal night,
  If it indeed may cleave its natal gloom,
Its doubtful promise thus I would unite
With thy belovèd name, thou Child of love and light.

II

The toil which stole from thee so many an hour,
  Is ended,—and the fruit is at thy feet!
No longer where the woods to frame a bower
  With interlacèd branches mix and meet,
  Or where with sound like many voices sweet,
Waterfalls leap among wild islands green,
  Which framed for my lone boat a lone retreat
Of moss-grown trees and weeds, shall I be seen:
But beside thee, where still my heart has ever been.

III

Thoughts of great deeds were mine, dear Friend, when
    first
    The clouds which wrap this world from youth did
      pass.
I do remember well the hour which burst
    My spirit's sleep: a fresh May-dawn it was,
    When I walked forth upon the glittering grass,
    And wept, I knew not why; until there rose
      From the near schoolroom, voices, that, alas!
    Were but one echo from a world of woes—
The harsh and grating strife of tyrants and of foes.

IV

And then I clasped my hands and looked around—
    —But none was near to mock my streaming eyes,
Which poured their warm drops on the sunny ground—
    So, without shame, I spake:—'I will be wise,
    And just, and free, and mild, if in me lies
Such power, for I grow weary to behold
    The selfish and the strong still tyrannise
Without reproach or check.' I then controlled
My tears, my heart grew calm, and I was meek and bold.

V

And from that hour did I with earnest thought
    Heap knowledge from forbidden mines of lore,
Yet nothing that my tyrants knew or taught
    I cared to learn, but from that secret store
    Wrought linkèd armour for my soul before
It might walk forth to war among mankind;
    Thus power and hope were strengthened more and
      more
Within me, till there came upon my mind
A sense of loneliness, a thirst with which I pined.

VI

Alas, that love should be a blight and snare
    To those who seek all sympathies in one!—
Such once I sought in vain; then black despair,
    The shadow of a starless night, was thrown
    Over the world in which I moved alone:—
Yet never found I one not false to me,
    Hard hearts, and cold, like weights of icy stone
Which crushed and withered mine, that could not be
Aught but a lifeless clod, until revived by thee.

VII

Thou Friend, those presence on my wintry heart
    Fell, like bright Spring upon some herbless plain;
How beautiful and calm and free thou wert
    In thy young wisdom, when the mortal chain
    Of Custom thou didst burst and rend in twain,
And walked as free as light the clouds among,
    Which many an envious slave then breathed in vain
From his dim dungeon, and my spirit sprung
To meet thee from the woes which had begirt it long!

VIII

No more alone through the world's wilderness,
    Although I trod the paths of high intent,
I journeyed now: no more companionless,
    Where solitude is like despair, I went.—
    There is the wisdom of a stern content
When Poverty can blight the just and good,
    When Infamy dares mock the innocent,
And cherished friends turn with the multitude
To trample: this was ours, and we unshaken stood!

IX

Now has descended a serener hour,
   And with inconstant fortune, friends return;
Though suffering leaves the knowledge and the power
   Which says:—Let scorn be not repaid with scorn.
   And from thy side two gentle babes are born
To fill our home with smiles, and thus are we
   Most fortunate beneath life's beaming morn;
And these delights, and thou, have been to me
The parents of the Song I consecrate to thee.

X

Is it, that now my inexperienced fingers
   But strike the prelude of a loftier strain?
Or, must the lyre on which my spirit lingers
   Soon pause in silence, ne'er to sound again,
   Though it might shake the Anarch Custom's reign,
And charm the minds of men to Truth's own sway
   Holier than was Amphion's? I would fain
Reply in hope—but I am worn away,
And Death and Love are yet contending for their prey.

XI

And what art thou? I know, but dare not speak:
   Time may interpret to his silent years.
Yet in the paleness of thy thoughtful cheek,
   And in the light thine ample forehead wears,
   And in thy sweetest smiles, and in thy tears,
And in thy gentle speech, a prophecy
   Is whispered, to subdue my fondest fears:
And through thine eyes, even in thy soul I see
A lamp of vestal fire burning internally.

XII

They say that thou wert lovely from thy birth,
   Of glorious parents, thou aspiring Child.
I wonder not—for One then left this earth
   Whose life was like a setting planet mild,
Which clothed thee in the radiance undefiled
   Of its departing glory; still her fame
   Shines on thee, through the tempests dark and wild
Which shake these latter days; and thou canst claim
The shelter, from thy Sire, of an immortal name.

XIII

One voice came forth from many a mighty spirit,
   Which was the echo of three thousand years;
And the tumultuous world stood mute to hear it,
   As some lone man who in a desert hears
   The music of his home:—unwonted fears
Fell on the pale oppressors of our race,
   And Faith, and Custom, and low-thoughted cares,
Like thunder-stricken dragons, for a space
Left the torn human heart, their food and dwelling-place.

XIV

Truth's deathless voice pauses among mankind!
   If there must be no response to my cry—
If men must rise and stamp with fury blind
   On his pure name who loves them,—thou and I,
   Sweet friend! can look from our tranquillity
Like lamps into the world's tempestuous night,—
   Two tranquil stars, while clouds are passing by
Which wrap them from the foundering seaman's sight,
That burn from year to year with unextinguished light.

Lines

I

The cold earth slept below,
   Above the cold sky shone;
And all around, with a chilling sound,
   From caves of ice and fields of snow,
   The breath of night like death did flow
     Beneath the sinking moon.

II

The wintry hedge was black,
   The green grass was not seen,
The birds did rest on the bare thorn's breast,
   Whose roots, beside the pathway track,
   Had bound their folds o'er many a crack
     Which the frost had made between.

III

Thine eyes glowed in the glare
   Of the moon's dying light;
As a fen-fire's beam on a sluggish stream
   Gleams dimly, so the moon shone there,
   And it yellowed the strings of thy raven hair,
     That shook in the wind of night.

IV

The moon made thy lips pale, beloved—
   The wind made thy bosom chill—
The night did shed on thy dear head
   Its frozen dew, and thou didst lie
   Where the bitter breath of the naked sky
     Might visit thee at will.

Song to the Men of England

I

Men of England, wherefore plough
For the lords who lay ye low?
Wherefore weave with toil and care
The rich robes your tyrants wear?

II

Wherefore feed, and clothe, and save,
From the cradle to the grave,
Those ungrateful drones who would
Drain your sweat—nay, drink your blood?

III

Wherefore, Bees of England, forge
Many a weapon, chain, and scourge,
That these stingless drones may spoil
The forced produce of your toil?

IV

Have ye leisure, comfort, calm,
Shelter, food, love's gentle balm?
Or what is it ye buy so dear
With your pain and with your fear?

V

The seed ye sow, another reaps;
The wealth ye find, another keeps;
The robes ye weave, another wears;
The arms ye forge, another bears.

VI

Sow seed,—but let no tyrant reap;
Find wealth,—let no imposter heap;

Weave robes,—let not the idle wear;
Forge arms,—in your defence to bear.

VII

Shrink to your cellars, holes, and cells;
In halls ye deck another dwells.
Why shake the chains ye wrought? Ye see
The steel ye tempered glance on ye.

VIII

With plough and spade, and hoe and loom,
Trace your grave, and build your tomb,
And weave your winding-sheet, till fair
England be your sepulchre.

Ozymandias

I met a traveller from an antique land
Who said: Two vast and trunkless legs of stone
Stand in the desert . . . Near them, on the sand,
Half sunk, a shattered visage lies, whose frown,
And wrinkled lip, and sneer of cold command,
Tell that its sculptor well those passions read
Which yet survive, stamped on these lifeless things,
The hand that mocked them, and the heart that fed:
And on the pedestal these words appear:
'My name is Ozymandias, king of kings:
Look on my works, ye Mighty, and despair!'
Nothing beside remains. Round the decay
Of that colossal wreck, boundless and bare
The lone and level sands stretch far away.

The Indian Serenade

I

I arise from dreams of thee
In the first sweet sleep of night.
When the winds are breathing low,
And the stars are shining bright:
I arise from dreams of thee,
And a spirit in my feet
Hath led me—who knows how?
To thy chamber window, Sweet!

II

The wandering airs they faint
On the dark, the silent stream—
The Champak odours fail
Like sweet thoughts in a dream;
The nightingale's complaint,
It dies upon her heart;—
As I must on thine,
Oh, belovèd as thou art!

III

Oh lift me from the grass!
I die! I faint! I fail!
Let thy love in kisses rain
On my lips and eyelids pale.
My cheek is cold and white, alas!
My heart beats loud and fast;—
Oh! press it to thine own again,
Where it will break at last.

Fragment: Thoughts Come and Go
in Solitude

My thoughts arise and fade in solitude,
  The verse that would invest them melts away
  Like moonlight in the heaven of spreading day:
How beautiful they were, how firm they stood,
Flecking the starry sky like woven pearl!

FROM *Alastor; or The Spirit of Solitude*

                        While daylight held
The sky, the Poet kept mute conference
With his still soul. At night the passion came,
Like the fierce fiend of a distempered dream,
And shook him from his rest, and led him forth
Into the darkness.—As an eagle grasped
In folds of the green serpent, feels her breast
Burn with the poison, and precipitates
Through night and day, tempest, and calm, and cloud,
Frantic with dizzying anguish, her blind flight
O'er the wide aëry wilderness: thus driven
By the bright shadow of that lovely dream,
Beneath the cold glare of the desolate night,
Through tangled swamps and deep precipitous dells,
Startling with careless step the moonlight snake,
He fled. Red morning dawned upon his flight,
Shedding the mockery of its vital hues
Upon his cheeks of death. He wandered on
Till vast Aornos seen from Petra's steep
Hung o'er the low horizon like a cloud;
Through Balk, and where the desolated tombs

Of Parthian kings scatter to every wind
Their wasting dust, wildly he wandered on,
Day after day a weary waste of hours,
Bearing within his life the brooding care
That ever fed on its decaying flame.
And now his limbs were lean; his scattered hair
Sered by the autumn of strange suffering
Sung dirges in the wind; his listless hand
Hung like dead bone within its withered skin;
Life, and the lustre that consumed it, shone
As in a furnace burning secretly
From his dark eyes alone. The cottagers,
Who ministered with human charity
His human wants, beheld with wondering awe
Their fleeting visitant. The mountaineer,
Encountering on some dizzy precipice
That spectral form, deemed that the Spirit of wind
With lightning eyes, and eager breath, and feet
Disturbing not the drifted snow, had paused
In its career: the infant would conceal
His troubled visage in his mother's robe
In terror at the glare of those wild eyes,
To remember their strange light in many a dream
Of after-times; but youthful maidens, taught
By nature, would interpret half the woe
That wasted him, would call him with false names
Brother, and friend, would press his pallid hand
At parting, and watch, dim through tears, the path
Of his departure from their father's door.

  At length upon the lone Chorasmian shore
He paused, a wide and melancholy waste
Of putrid marshes. A strong impulse urged
His steps to the sea-shore. A swan was there,
Beside a sluggish stream among the reeds.

It rose as he approached, and with strong wings
Scaling the upward sky, bent its bright course
High over the immeasurable main.
His eyes pursued its flight.—'Thou hast a home,
Beautiful bird; thou voyagest to thine home,
Where thy sweet mate will twine her downy neck
With thine, and welcome thy return with eyes
Bright in the luste of their own fond joy.
And what am I that I should linger here,
With voice far sweeter than thy dying notes,
Spirit more vast than thine, frame more attuned
To beauty, wasting these surpassing powers
In the deaf air, to the blind earth, and heaven
That echoes not my thoughts?' A gloomy smile
Of desperate hope wrinkled his quivering lips.
For sleep, he knew, kept most relentlessly
Its precious charge, and silent death exposed,
Faithless perhaps as sleep, a shadowy lure,
With doubtful smile mocking its own strange charms.

Startled by his own thoughts he looked around.
There was no fair fiend near him, not a sight
Or sound of awe but in his own deep mind.
A little shallop floating near the shore
Caught the impatient wandering of his gaze.
It had been long abandoned, for its sides
Gaped wide with many a rift, and its frail joints
Swayed with the undulations of the tide.
A restless impulse urged him to embark
And meet lone Death on the drear ocean's waste;
For well he knew that mighty Shadow loves
The slimy caverns of the populous deep.

The day was fair and sunny, sea and sky
Drank its inspiring radiance, and the wind

Swept strongly from the shore, blackening the waves.
Following his eager soul, the wanderer
Leaped in the boat, he spread his cloak aloft
On the bare mast, and took his lonely seat,
And felt the boat speed o'er the tranquil sea
Like a torn cloud before the hurricane.

   As one that in a silver vision floats
Obedient to the sweep of odorous winds
Upon resplendent clouds, so rapidly
Along the dark and ruffled waters fled
The straining boat.—A whirlwind swept it on,
With fierce gusts and precipitating force,
Through the white ridges of the chafèd sea.
The waves arose. Higher and higher still
Their fierce necks writhed beneath the tempest's scourge
Like serpents struggling in a vulture's grasp.
Calm and rejoicing in the fearful war
Of wave ruining on wave, and blast on blast
Descending, and black flood on whirlpool driven
With dark obliterating course, he sate:
As if their genii were the ministers
Appointed to conduct him to the light
Of those belovèd eyes, the Poet sate
Holding the steady helm. Evening came on,
The beams of sunset hung their rainbow hues
High 'mid the shifting domes of sheeted spray
That canopied his path o'er the waste deep;
Twilight, ascending slowly from the east,
Entwined in duskier wreaths her braided locks
O'er the fair front and radiant eyes of day;
Night followed, clad with stars. On every side
More horribly the multitudinous streams
Of ocean's mountainous waste to mutual war
Rushed in dark tumult thundering, as to mock

The calm and spangled sky. The little boat
Still fled before the storm; still fled, like foam
Down the steep cataract of a wintry river;
Now pausing on the edge of the riven wave;
Now leaving far behind the bursting mass
That fell, convulsing ocean: safely fled—
As if that frail and wasted human form,
Had been an elemental god.

                  At midnight
The moon arose: and lo! the ethereal cliffs
Of Caucasus, whose icy summits shone
Among the stars like sunlight, and around
Whose caverned base the whirlpools and the waves
Bursting and eddying irresistibly
Rage and resound for ever.—Who shall save?—
The boat fled on,—the boiling torrent drove,—
The crags closed round with black and jaggèd arms,
The shattered mountain overhung the sea,
And faster still, beyond all human speed,
Suspended on the sweep of the smooth wave,
The little boat was driven. A cavern there
Yawned, and amid its slant and winding depths
Ingulfed the rushing sea. The boat fled on
With unrelaxing speed.—'Vision and Love!'
The Poet cried aloud, 'I have beheld
The path of thy departure. Sleep and death
Shall not divide us long!'

Song

I

Rarely, rarely, comest thou,
   Spirit of Delight!

Wherefore hast thou left me now
   Many a day and night?
Many a weary night and day
'Tis since thou art fled away.

II

How shall ever one like me
   Win thee back again?
With the joyous and the free
   Thou wilt scoff at pain.
Spirit false! thou hast forgot
   All but those who need thee not.

III

As a lizard with the shade
   Of a trembling leaf,
Thou with sorrow art dismayed;
   Even the sighs of grief
Reproach thee, that thou art not near,
And reproach thou wilt not hear.

IV

Let me set my mournful ditty
   To a merry measure;
Thou wilt never come for pity,
   Thou wilt come for pleasure;
   Pity then will cut away
Those cruel wings, and thou wilt stay.

V

I love all that thou lovest,
   Spirit of Delight!
The fresh Earth in new leaves dressed,
   And the starry night;

Autumn evening, and the morn
When the golden mists are born.

VI

I love snow, and all the forms
   Of the radiant frost;
I love waves, and winds, and storms,
   Everything almost
Which is Nature's, and may be
Untainted by man's misery.

VII

I love tranquil solitude,
   And such society
As is quiet, wise, and good;
   Between thee and me
What difference? but thou dost possess
The things I seek, not love them less.

VIII

I love Love—though he has wings,
   And like light can flee,
But above all other things,
   Spirit, I love thee—
Thou are love and life! Oh, come,
Make once more my heart thy home.

To——

Music, when soft voices die,
Vibrates in the memory—
Odours, when sweet violets sicken,
Live within the sense they quicken.

[34]

Rose leaves, when the rose is dead,
Are heaped for the belovèd's bed;
And so thy thoughts, when thou art gone,
Love itself shall slumber on.

Fragment: 'Is it that in some brighter sphere'

Is it that in some brighter sphere
We part from friends we meet with here?
Or do we see the Future pass
Over the Present's dusky glass?

Or what is that that makes us seem
To patch up fragments of a dream,
Part of which comes true, and part
Beats and trembles in the heart?

Lines Written among Euganean Hills

OCTOBER, 1818

Many a green isle needs must be
In the deep wide sea of Misery,
Or the mariner, worn and wan,
Never thus could voyage on—
Day and night, and night and day,
Drifting on his dreary way,
With the solid darkness black
Closing round his vessel's track;
Whilst above the sunless sky,
Big with clouds, hangs heavily,
And behind the tempest fleet

Hurries on with lightning feet,
Riving sail, and cord, and plank,
Till the ship has almost drank
Death from the o'er-brimming deep;
And sinks down, down, like that sleep
When the dreamer seems to be
Weltering through eternity;
And the dim low line before
Of a dark and distant shore
Still recedes, as ever still
Longing with divided will,
But no power to seek or shun,
He is ever drifted on
O'er the unreposing wave
To the haven of the grave.

What, if there no friends will greet;
What, if there no heart will meet
His with love's impatient beat;
Wander wheresoe'er he may,
Can he dream before that day
To find refuge from distress
In friendship's smile, in love's caress?
Then 'twill wreak him little woe
Whether such there be or no:
Senseless is the breast, and cold,
Which relenting love would fold;
Bloodless are the veins and chill
Which the pulse of pain did fill;
Every little living nerve
That from bitter words did swerve
Round the tortured lips and brow,
Are like sapless leaflets now
Frozen upon December's bough.

On the beach of a northern sea
Which tempests shake eternally,
As once the wretch there lay to sleep,
Lies a solitary heap,
One white skull and seven dry bones,
On the margin of the stones,
Where a few gray rushes stand,
Boundaries of the sea and land:
Nor is heard one voice of wail
But the sea-mews, as they sail
O'er the billows of the gale;
Or the whirlwind up and down
Howling, like a slaughtered town,
When a king in glory rides
Through the pomp of fratricides:
Those unburied bones around
There is many a mournful sound;
There is no lament for him,
Like a sunless vapour, dim,
Who once clothed with life and thought
What now moves nor murmurs not.

Ay, many flowering islands lie
In the waters of wide Agony:
To such a one this morn was led,
My bark by soft winds piloted:
'Mid the mountains Euganean
I stood listening to the paean
With which the legioned rooks did hail
The sun's uprise majestical;
Gathering round with wings all hoar,
Through the dewy mist they soar
Like gray shades, till the eastern heaven
Bursts, and then, as clouds of even,
Flecked with fire and azure, lie

In the unfathomable sky,
So their plumes of purple grain,
Starred with drops of golden rain,
Gleam above the sunlight woods,
As in silent multitudes
On the morning's fitful gale
Through the broken mist they sail,
And the vapours cloven and gleaming
Follow, down the dark steep streaming,
Till all is bright, and clear, and still,
Round the solitary hill.

Beneath is spread like a green sea
The waveless plain of Lombardy,
Bounded by the vaporous air,
Islanded by cities fair;
Underneath Day's azure eyes
Ocean's nursling, Venice lies,
A peopled labyrinth of walls,
Amphitrite's destined halls,
Which her hoary sire now paves
With his blue and beaming waves.
Lo! the sun upsprings behind,
Broad, red, radiant, half-reclined
On the level quivering line
Of the waters crystalline;
And before that chasm of light,
As within a furnace bright,
Column, tower, and dome, and spire,
Shine like obelisks of fire,
Pointing with inconstant motion
From the altar of dark ocean
To the sapphire-tinted skies;
As the flames of sacrifice
From the marble shrines did rise,

As to pierce the dome of gold
Where Apollo spoke of old.

Sun-girt City, thou hast been
Ocean's child, and then his queen;
Now is come a darker day,
And thou soon must be his prey,
If the power that raised thee here
Hallow so thy watery bier.
A less drear ruin then than now,
With thy conquest-branded brow
Stooping to the slave of slaves
From thy throne, among the waves
Wilt thou be, when the sea-mew
Flies, as once before it flew,
O'er thine isles depopulate,
And all is in its ancient state,
Save where many a palace gate
With green sea-flowers overgrown
Like a rock of Ocean's own,
Topples o'er the abandoned sea
As the tides change sullenly.
The fisher on his watery way,
Wandering at the close of day,
Will spread his sail and seize his oar
Till he pass the gloomy shore,
Lest thy dead should, from their sleep
Bursting o'er the starlight deep,
Lead a rapid masque of death
O'er the waters of his path.

Those who alone thy towers behold
Quivering through aëreal gold,
As I now behold them here,
Would imagine not they were

Sepulchres, where human forms,
Like pollution-nourished worms,
To the corpse of greatness cling,
Murdered, and now mouldering:
But if Freedom should awake
In her omnipotence, and shake
From the Celtic Anarch's hold
All the keys of dungeons cold,
Where a hundred cities lie
Chained like thee, ingloriously,
Thou and all thy sister band
Might adorn this sunny land,
Twining memories of old time
With new virtues more sublime;
If not, perish thou and they!—
Clouds which stain truth's rising day
By her sun consumed away—
Earth can spare ye: while like flowers,
In the waste of years and hours,
From your dust new nations spring
With more kindly blossoming.

Perish—let there only be
Floating o'er thy heartless sea
As the garment of thy sky
Clothes the world immortally,
One remembrance, more sublime
Than the tattered pall of time,
Which scarce hides thy visage wan;—
That a tempest-cleaving Swan
Of the songs of Albion,
Driven from his ancestral streams
By the might of evil dreams,
Found a nest in thee; and Ocean
Welcomed him with such emotion

That its joy grew his, and sprung
From his lips like music flung
O'er a mighty thunder-fit,
Chastening terror:—what though yet
Poesy's unfailing River,
Which through Albion winds forever
Lashing with melodious wave
Many a sacred Poet's grave,
Mourn its latest nursling fled?
What though thou with all thy dead
Scarce can for this fame repay
Aught thine own? oh, rather say
Though thy sins and slaveries foul
Overcloud a sunlike soul?
As the ghost of Homer clings
Round Scamander's wasting springs;
As divinest Shakespeare's might
Fills Avon and the world with light
Like omniscient power which he
Imaged 'mid mortality;
As the love from Petrarch's urn,
Yet amid yon hills doth burn,
A quenchless lamp by which the heart
See things unearthly;—so thou art,
Mighty spirit—so shall be
The City that did refuge thee.

Lo, the sun floats up the sky
Like thought-wingèd Liberty,
Till the universal light
Seems to level plain and height;
From the sea a mist has spread,
And the beams of morn lie dead
On the towers of Venice now,
Like its glory long ago.

By the skirts of that gray cloud
Many-domèd Padua proud
Stands, a peopled solitude,
'Mid the harvest-shining plain,
Where the peasant heaps his grain
In the garner of his foe,
And the milk-white oxen slow
With the purple vintage strain,
Heaped upon the creaking wain,
That the brutal Celt may swill
Drunken sleep with savage will;
And the sickle to the sword
Lies unchanged, though many a lord,
Like a weed whose shade is poison,
Overgrows this region's foison,
Sheaves of whom are ripe to come
To destruction's harvest-home:
Men must reap the things they sow,
Force from force must ever flow,
Or worse; but 'tis a bitter woe
That love or reason cannot change
The despot's rage, the slave's revenge.

Padua, thou within whose walls
Those mute guests at festivals,
Son and Mother, Death and Sin,
Played at dice for Ezzelin,
Till Death cried, 'I win, I win!'
And Sin cursed to lose the wager,
But Death promised, to assuage her,
That he would petition for
Her to be made Vice-Emperor,
When the destined years were o'er,
Over all between the Po
And the eastern Alpine snow,

Under the mighty Austrian.
Sin smiled so as Sin only can,
And since that time, ay, long before,
Both have ruled from shore to shore,—
That incestuous pair, who follow
Tyrants as the sun the swallow,
As Repentance follows Crime,
And as changes follow Time.

In thine halls the lamp of learning,
Padua, now no more is burning;
Like a meteor, whose wild way
Is lost over the grave of day,
It gleams betrayed and to betray:
Once remotest nations came
To adore that sacred flame,
When it lit not many a hearth
On this cold and gloomy earth:
Now new fires from antique light
Spring beneath the wide world's might;
But their spark lies dead in thee,
Trampled out by Tyranny.
As the Norway woodman quells,
In the depth of piny dells,
One light flame among the brakes,
While the boundless forest shakes,
And its mighty trunks are torn
By the fire thus lowly born:
The spark beneath his feet is dead,
He starts to see the flames it fed
Howling through the darkened sky
With a myriad tongues victoriously,
And sinks down in fear: so thou,
O Tyranny, beholdest now
Light around thee, and thou hearest

The loud flames ascend, and fearest:
Grovel on the earth; ay, hide
In the dust thy purple pride!

Noon descends around me now:
'Tis the noon of autumn's glow,
When a soft and purple mist
Like a vaporous amethyst,
Or an air-dissolvèd star
Mingling light and fragrance, far
From the curved horizon's bound
To the point of Heaven's profound,
Fills the overflowing sky;
And the plains that silent lie
Underneath, the leaves unsodden
Where the infant Frost has trodden
With his morning-winged feet,
Whose bright print is gleaming yet:
And the red and golden vines,
Piercing with their trellised lines
The rough, dark-skirted wilderness;
The dun and bladed grass no less,
Pointing from his hoary tower
In the windless air; the flower
Glimmering at my feet; the line
Of the olive-sandalled Apennine
In the south dimly islanded;
And the Alps, whose snows are spread
High between the clouds and sun;
And of living things each one;
And my spirit which so long
Darkened this swift stream of song,—
Interpenetrated lie
By the glory of the sky:
Be it love, light, harmony,

Odour, or the soul of all
Which from Heaven like dew doth fall,
Or the mind which feeds this verse
Peopling the lone universe.

Noon descends, and after noon
Autumn's evening meets me soon,
Leading the infantine moon,
And that one star, which to her
Almost seems to minister
Half the crimson light she brings
From the sunset's radiant springs:
And the soft dreams of the morn
(Which like wingèd winds had borne
To that silent isle, which lies
Mid remembered agonies,
The frail bark of this lone being)
Pass, to other sufferers fleeing,
And its ancient pilot, Pain,
Sits beside the helm again.

Other flowering isles must be
In the sea of Life and Agony:
Other spirits float and flee
O'er that gulf: even now, perhaps,
On some rock the wild wave wraps,
With folded wings they waiting sit
For my bark, to pilot it
To some calm and blooming cove,
Where for me, and those I love,
May a windless bower be built,
Far from passion, pain, and guilt,
In a dell mid lawny hills,
Which the wild sea-murmur fills,
And soft sunshine, and the sound

Of old forests echoing round,
And the light and smell divine
Of all flowers that breathe and shine:
We may live so happy there,
That the Spirits of the Air,
Envying us, may even entice
To our healing Paradise
The polluting multitude;
But their rage would be subdued
By that clime divine and calm,
And the winds whose wings rain balm
On the uplifted soul, and leaves
Under which the bright sea heaves;
While each breathless interval
In their whisperings musical
The inspired soul supplies
With its own deep melodies,
And the love which heals all strife
Circling, like the breath of life,
All things in that sweet abode
With its own mild brotherhood:
They, not it, would change; and soon
Every sprite beneath the moon
Would repent its envy vain,
And the earth grow young again.

Ode to the West Wind[1]

1 This poem was conceived and chiefly written in a wood that skirts
the Arno, near Florence, and on a day when that tempestuous wind,
whose temperature is at once mild and animating, was collecting the
vapours which pour down the autumnal rains. They began, as I fore-
saw, at sunset with a violent tempest of hail and rain, attended by that
magnificent thunder and lightning peculiar to the Cisalpine regions.

I

O wild West Wind, thou breath of Autumn's being,
Thou, from whose unseen presence the leaves dead
Are driven, like ghosts from an enchanter fleeing,

Yellow, and black, and pale, and hectic red,
Pestilence-stricken multitudes: O thou,
Who chariotest to their dark wintry bed

The wingèd seeds, where they lie cold and low,
Each like a corpse within its grave, until
Thine azure sister of the Spring shall blow

Her clarion o'er the dreaming earth, and fill
(Driving sweet buds like flocks to feed in air)
With living hues and odours plain and hill:

Wild Spirit, which art moving everywhere;
Destroyer and preserver; hear, oh, hear!

II

Thou on whose stream, mid the steep sky's commotion,
Loose clouds like earth's decaying leaves are shed,
Shook from the tangled boughs of Heaven and Ocean,

Angels of rain and lightning: there are spread
On the blue surface of thine aëry surge,
Like the bright hair uplifted from the head

Of some fierce Maenad, even from the dim verge

The phenomenon alluded to at the conclusion of the third stanza is
well known to naturalists. The vegetation at the bottom of the sea, of
rivers, and of lakes, sympathizes with that of the land in the change of
seasons, and is consequently influenced by the winds which announce
it.—[SHELLEY'S NOTE.]

Of the horizon to the zenith's height,
The locks of the approaching storm. Thou dirge

Of the dying year, to which this closing night
Will be the dome of a vast sepulchre,
Vaulted with all thy congregated might

Of vapours, from whose solid atmosphere
Black rain, and fire, and hail will burst: oh, hear!

III

Thou who didst waken from his summer dreams
The blue Mediterranean, where he lay,
Lulled by the coil of his crystalline streams,

Beside a pumice isle in Baiae's bay,
And saw in sleep old palaces and towers
Quivering within the wave's intenser day,

All overgrown with azure moss and flowers
So sweet, the sense faints picturing them! Thou
For whose path the Atlantic's level powers

Cleave themselves into chasms, while far below
The sea-blooms and the oozy woods which wear
The sapless foliage of the ocean, know

Thy voice, and suddenly grow gray with fear,
And tremble and despoil themselves: oh, hear!

IV

If I were a dead leaf thou mightest bear;
If I were a swift cloud to fly with thee;
A wave to pant beneath thy power, and share

The impulse of thy strength, only less free
Than thou, O uncontrollable! If even
I were as in my boyhood, and could be

The comrade of thy wanderings over Heaven,
As then, when to outstrip thy skiey speed
Scarce seemed a vision; I would ne'er have striven

As thus with thee in prayer in my sore need.
Oh, lift me as a wave, a leaf, a cloud!
I fall upon the thorns of life! I bleed!

A heavy weight of hours has chained and bowed
One too like thee: tameless, and swift, and proud.

V

Make me thy lyre, even as the forest is:
What if my leaves are falling like its own!
The tumult of thy mighty harmonies

Will take from both a deep, autumnal tone,
Sweet though in sadness. Be thou, Spirit fierce,
My spirit! Be thou me, impetuous one!

Drive my dead thoughts over the universe
Like withered leaves to quicken a new birth!
And, by the incantation of this verse,

Scatter, as from an unextinguished hearth
Ashes and sparks, my words among mankind!
Be through my lips to unawakened earth

The trumpet of a prophecy! O, Wind,
If Winter comes, can Spring be far behind?

FROM *Prometheus Unbound*

The Earth

Ere Babylon was dust,
The Magus Zoroaster, my dead child,
Met his own image walking in the garden.
That apparition, sole of men, he saw.
For know there are two worlds of life and death:
One that which thou beholdest; but the other
Is underneath the grave, where do inhabit
The shadows of all forms that think and live
Till death unite them and they part no more;
Dreams and the light imaginings of men,
And all that faith creates or love desires,
Terrible, strange, sublime and beauteous shapes.
There thou art, and dost hang, a writhing shade,
'Mid whirlwind-peopled mountains; all the gods
Are there, and all the powers of nameless worlds,
Vast, sceptred phantoms; heroes, men, and beasts;
And Demogorgon, a tremendous gloom;
And he, the supreme Tyrant, on his throne
Of burning gold. Son, one of these shall utter
The curse which all remember. Call at will
Thine own ghost, or the ghost of Jupiter,
Hades or Typhon, or what mightier Gods
From all-prolific Evil, since thy ruin
Have sprung, and trampled on my prostrate sons.
Ask, and they must reply: so the revenge
Of the Supreme may sweep through vacant shades,
As rainy wind through the abandoned gate
Of a fallen palace.

FROM *Prometheus Unbound*

Chorus of Spirits

From unremembered ages we
Gentle guides and guardians be
Of heaven-oppressed mortality;
And we breathe, and sicken not,
The atmosphere of human thought:
Be it dim, and dank, and gray,
Like a storm-extinguished day,
Travelled o'er by dying gleams;
   Be it bright as all between
Cloudless skies and windless streams,
   Silent, liquid, and serene;
As the birds within the wind,
   As the fish within the wave,
As the thoughts of man's own mind
   Float through all above the grave;
We make there our liquid lair,
Voyaging cloudlike and unpent
Through the boundless element:
Thence we bear the prophecy
Which begins and ends in thee!

Ione. More yet come, one by one: the air around them
Looks radiant as the air around a star.

First Spirit

On a battle-trumpet's blast
I fled hither, fast, fast, fast,
'Mid the darkness upward cast.
From the dust of creeds outworn,
From the tyrant's banner torn,
Gathering 'round me, onward borne,
There was mingled many a cry—

[51]

Freedom! Hope! Death! Victory!
Till they faded through the sky;
And one sound, above, around,
One sound beneath, around, above,
Was moving; 'twas the soul of Love;
'Twas the hope, the prophecy,
Which begins and ends in thee.

Second Spirit

A rainbow's arch stood on the sea,
Which rocked beneath, immovably;
And the triumphant storm did flee,
Like a conqueror, swift and proud,
Between, with many a captive cloud,
A shapeless, dark and rapid crowd,
Each by lightning riven in half:
I heard the thunder hoarsely laugh:
Mighty fleets were strewn like chaff
And spread beneath a hell of death
O'er the white waters. I alit
On a great ship lightning-split,
And speeded hither on the sigh
Of one who gave an enemy
His plank, then plunged aside to die.

Third Spirit

I sate beside a sage's bed,
And the lamp was burning red
Near the book where he had fed,
When a Dream with plumes of flame
To his pillow hovering came,
And I knew it was the same
Which had kindled long ago
Pity, eloquence, and woe;
And the world awhile below

Wore the shade, its lustre made.
It has borne me here as fleet
As Desire's lightning feet:
I must ride it back ere morrow,
Or the sage will wake in sorrow.

Fourth Spirit

On a poet's lips I slept
Dreaming like a love-adept
In the sound his breathing kept;
Nor seeks nor finds he mortal blisses,
But feeds on the aëreal kisses
Of shapes that haunt thought's wildernesses.
He will watch from dawn to gloom
The lake-reflected sun illume
The yellow bees in the ivy-bloom,
Nor heed nor see, what things they be;
But from these create he can
Forms more real than living man,
Nurslings of immortality!
One of these awakened me,
And I sped to succour thee.

FROM *Prometheus Unbound*

FROM ACT TWO

Asia

Who reigns? There was the Heaven and Earth at first,
And Light and Love; then Saturn, from whose throne
Time fell, an envious shadow: such the state
Of the earth's primal spirits beneath his sway,
As the calm joy of flowers and living leaves
Before the wind or sun has withered them

[53]

And semivital worms; but he refused
The birthright of their being, knowledge, power,
The skill which wields the elements, the thought
Which pierces this dim universe like light,
Self-empire, and the majesty of love;
For thirst of which they fainted. Then Prometheus
Gave wisdom, which is strength, to Jupiter,
And with this law alone, 'Let man be free,'
Clothed him with the dominion of wide Heaven.
To know nor faith, nor love, nor law; to be
Omnipotent but friendless is to reign;
And Jove now reigned; for on the race of man
First famine, and then toil, and then disease,
Strife, wounds, and ghastly death unseen before,
Fell; and the unseasonable seasons drove
With alternating shafts of frost and fire,
Their shelterless, pale tribes to mountain caves:
And in their desert hearts fierce wants he sent,
And mad disquietudes, and shadows idle
Of unreal good, which levied mutual war,
So ruining the lair wherein they raged.
Prometheus saw, and waked the legioned hopes
Which sleep within folded Elysian flowers,
Nepenthe, Moly, Amaranth, fadeless blooms,
That they might hide with thin and rainbow wings
The shape of Death; and Love he sent to bind
The disunited tendrils of that vine
Which bears the wine of life, the human heart;
And he tamed fire which, like some beast of prey,
Most terrible, but lovely, played beneath
The frown of man; and tortured to his will
Iron and gold, the slaves and signs of power,
And gems and poisons, and all subtlest forms
Hidden beneath the mountains and the waves.
He gave man speech, and speech created thought,

Which is the measure of the universe;
And Science struck the thrones of earth and heaven,
Which shook, but fell not; and the harmonious mind
Poured itself forth in all-prophetic song;
And music lifted up the listening spirit
Until it walked, exempt from mortal care.
Godlike, o'er the clear billows of sweet sound;
And human hands first mimicked and then mocked,
With moulded limbs more lovely than its own,
The human form, till marble grew divine;
And mothers, gazing, drank the love men see
Reflected in their race, behold, and perish.
He told the hidden power of herbs and springs,
And Disease drank and slept. Death grew like sleep.
He taught the implicated orbits woven
Of the wide-wandering stars; and how the sun
Changes his lair, and by what secret spell
The pale moon is transformed, when her broad eye
Gazes not on the interlunar sea:
He taught to rule, as life directs the limbs,
The tempest-wingèd chariots of the Ocean,
And the Celt knew the Indian. Cities then
Were built, and through their snow-like column flowed
The warm winds, and the azure aether shone,
And the blue sea and shadowy hills were seen.
Such, the alleviations of his state,
Prometheus gave to man, for which he hangs
Withering in destined pain: but who rains down
Evil, the immedicable plague, which, while
Man looks on his creation like a God
And sees that it is glorious, drives him on,
The wreck of his own will, the scorn of earth,
The outcast, the abandoned, the alone?
Not Jove: while yet his frown shook Heaven, ay, when
His adversary from adamantine chains

Cursed him, he trembled like a slave. Declare
Who is his master? Is he too a slave?

FROM *Prometheus Unbound*

FROM ACT THREE
Spirit of the Hour
Soon as the sound had ceased whose thunder filled
The abysses of the sky and the wide earth,
There was a change: the impalpable thin air
And the all-circling sunlight were transformed,
As if the sense of love dissolved in them
Had folded itself round the sphered world.
My vision then grew clear, and I could see
Into the mysteries of the universe:
Dizzy as with delight I floated down,
Winnowing the lightsome air with languid plumes,
My courses sought their birthplace in the sun,
Where they henceforth will live exempt from toil,
Pasturing flowers of vegetable fire;
And where my moonlike car will stand within
A temple, gazed upon by Phidian forms
Of thee, and Asia, and the Earth, and me,
And you fair nymphs looking the love we feel,—
In memory of the tidings it has borne,—
Beneath a dome fretted with graven flowers,
Poised on twelve colums of resplendent stone,
And open to the bright and liquid sky.
Yoked to it by an amphisbaenic snake
The likeness of those wingèd steeds will mock
The flight from which they find repose. Alas,
Whither has wandered now my partial tongue
When all remains untold which ye would hear?

As I have said, I floated to the earth:
It was, as it is still, the pain of bliss
To move, to breathe, to be; I wandering went
Among the haunts and dwellings of mankind,
And first was disappointed not to see
Such mighty change as I had felt within
Expressed in outward things; but soon I looked,
And behold, thrones were kingless, and men walked
One with the other even as spirits do,
None fawned, none trampled; hate, disdain, or fear,
Self-love or self-contempt, on human brows
No more inscribed, as o'er the gate of hell,
'All hope abandon ye who enter here;'
None frowned, none trembled, none with eager fear
Gazed on another's eye of cold command,
Until the subject of a tyrant's will
Became, worse fate, the abject of his own,
Which spurred him, like an outspent horse, to death.
None wrought his lips in truth-entangling lines
Which smiled the lie his tongue disdained to speak;
None, with firm sneer, trod out in his own heart
The sparks of love and hope till there remained
Those bitter ashes, a soul self-consumed,
And the wretch crept a vampire among men,
Infecting all with his own hideous ill;
None talked that common, false, cold, hollow talk
Which makes the heart deny the *yes* it breathes,
Yet question that unmeant hypocrisy
With such a self-mistrust as has no name.
And women, too, frank, beautiful, and kind
As the free heaven which rains fresh light and dew
On the wide earth, past; gentle radiant forms,
From custom's evil taint exempt and pure;
Speaking the wisdom once they could not think,
Looking emotions once they feared to feel,

And changed to all which once they dared not be,
Yet being now, made earth like heaven; nor pride,
Nor jealousy, nor envy, nor ill shame,
The bitterest of those drops of treasured gall,
Spoilt the sweet taste of the nepenthe, love.

Thrones, altars, judgement-seats, and prisons; wherein,
And beside which, by wretched men were borne
Sceptres, tiaras, swords, and chains, and tomes
Of reasoned wrong, glozed on by ignorance,
Were like those monstrous and barbaric shapes,
The ghosts of a no-more-remembered fame,
Which, from their unworn obelisks, look forth
In triumph o'er the palaces and tombs
Of those who were their conquerors: mouldering round,
These imaged to the pride of kings and priests
A dark yet mighty faith, a power as wide
As is the world it wasted, and are now
But an astonishment; even so the tools
And emblems of its last captivity,
Amid the dwellings of the peopled earth,
Stand, not o'erthrown, but unregarded now.
And those foul shapes, abhorred by god and man,—
Which, under many a name and many a form
Strange, savage, ghastly, dark and execrable,
Were Jupiter, the tyrant of the world;
And which the nations, panic-stricken, served
With blood, and hearts broken by long hope, and love
Dragged to his altars soiled and garlandless,
And slain amid men's unreclaiming tears,
Flattering the thing they feared, which fear was hate,—
Frown, mouldering fast, o'er their abandoned shrines:
The painted veil, by those who were, called life,
Which mimicked, as with colours idly spread,
All men believed or hoped, is torn aside;

The loathsome mask has fallen, the man remains
Sceptreless, free, uncircumscribed, but man
Equal, unclassed, tribeless, and nationless,
Exempt from awe, worship, degree, the king
Over himself; just, gentle, wise: but man
Passionless?——no, yet free from guilt or pain,
Which were, for his will made or suffered them,
Nor yet exempt, though ruling them like slaves,
From chance, and death, and mutability,
The clogs of that which else might oversoar
The loftiest star of unascended heaven,
Pinnacled dim in the intense inane.

Love's Philosophy

I

The fountains mingle with the river
    And the rivers with the Ocean,
The winds of Heaven mix for ever
    With a sweet emotion;
Nothing in the world is single;
    All things by a law divine
In one spirit meet and mingle.
    Why not I with thine?—

II

See the mountains kiss high Heaven
    And the waves clasp one another;
No sister-flower would be forgiven
    If it disdained its brother;
And the sunlight clasps the earth
    And the moonbeams kiss the sea:
What is all this sweet work worth
    If thou kiss not me?

The Cloud

I bring fresh showers for the thirsting flowers,
    From the seas and the streams;
I bear light shade for the leaves when laid
    In their noonday dreams.
From my wings are shaken the dews that waken
    The sweet buds every one,
When rocked to rest on their mother's breast,
    As she dances about the sun.
I wield the flail of the lashing hail,
    And whiten the green plains under,
And then again I dissolve it in rain,
    And laugh as I pass in thunder.

I sift the snow on the mountains below,
    And their great pines groan aghast;
And all the night 'tis my pillow white,
    While I sleep in the arms of the blast.
Sublime on the towers of my skiey bowers,
    Lightning my pilot sits;
In a cavern under is fettered the thunder,
    It struggles and howls at fits;
Over earth and ocean, with gentle motion,
    This pilot is guiding me,
Lured by the love of the genii that move
    In the depths of the purple sea;
Over the rills, and the crags, and the hills,
    Over the lakes and the plains,
Wherever he dream, under mountain or stream,
    The Spirit he loves remains;
And I all the while bask in Heaven's blue smile,
    Whilst he is dissolving in rains.

The sanguine Sunrise, with his meteor eyes,

And his burning plumes outspread,
Leaps on the back of my sailing rack,
    When the morning star shines dead;
As on the jag of a mountain crag,
    Which an earthquake rocks and swings,
An eagle alit one moment may sit
  In the light of its golden wings.
And when Sunset may breathe, from the lit sea beneath,
    Its ardours of rest and of love,
And the crimson pall of eve may fall
    From the depth of Heaven above,
With wings folded I rest, on mine aëry nest,
    As still as a brooding dove.

That orbèd maiden with white fire laden,
    Whom mortals call the Moon,
Glides glimmering o'er my fleece-like floor,
    By the midnight breezes strewn;
And wherever the beat of her unseen feet,
    Which only the angels hear,
May have broken the woof of my tent's thin roof,
    The stars peep behind her and peer;
And I laugh to see them whirl and flee,
    Like a swarm of golden bees,
When I widen the rent in my wind-built tent,
    Till the calm rivers, lakes, and seas,
Like strips of the sky fallen through me on high,
    Are each paved with the moon and these.

I bind the Sun's throne with a burning zone,
    And the Moon's with a girdle of pearl;
The volcanoes are dim, and the stars reel and swim,
    When the whirlwinds my banner unfurl.
From cape to cape, with a bridge-like shape,
    Over a torrent sea,

Sunbeam-proof, I hang like a roof,—
    The mountains its columns be.
The triumphal arch through which I march
    With hurricane, fire, and snow,
When the Powers of the air are chained to my chair,
    Is the million-coloured bow;
The sphere-fire above its soft colours wove,
    While the moist Earth was laughing below.

I am the daughter of Earth and Water,
    And the nursling of the Sky;
I pass through the pores of the ocean and shores;
    I change, but I cannot die.
For after the rain when with never a stain
    The pavilion of Heaven is bare,
And the winds and sunbeams with their convex gleams
    Build up the blue dome of air,
I silently laugh at my own cenotaph,
    And out of the caverns of rain,
Like a child from the womb, like a ghost from the tomb
    I arise and unbuild it again.

To Jane: the Recollection

I

Now the last day of many days,
    All beautiful and bright as thou,
        The loveliest and the last, is dead,
Rise, Memory, and write its praise!
    Up,—to thy wonted work! come, trace
        The epitaph of glory fled,—
For now the Earth has changed its face,
    A frown is on the Heaven's brow.

II

We wandered to the Pine Forest
   That skirts the Ocean's foam,
The lightest wind was in its nest,
   The tempest in its home.
The whispering waves were half asleep,
   The clouds were gone to play,
And on the bosom of the deep
   The smile of Heaven lay;
It seemed as if the hour were one
   Sent from beyond the skies,
Which scattered from above the sun
   A light of Paradise.

III

We paused amid the pines that stood
   The giants of the waste,
Tortured by storms to shapes as rude
   As serpents interlaced,
And soothed by every azure breath,
   That under Heaven is blown,
To harmonies and hues beneath,
   As tender as its own;
Now all the tree-tops lay asleep,
   Like green waves on the sea,
As still as in the silent deep
   The ocean woods may be.

IV

How calm it was!—the silence there
   By such a chain was bound
That even the busy woodpecker
   Made stiller by her sound
The inviolable quietness;
   The breath of peace we drew

With its soft motion made not less
   The calm that round us grew.
There seemed from the remotest seat
   Of the white mountain waste,
To the soft flower beneath our feet,
   A magic circle traced,—
A spirit interfused around,
   A thrilling, silent life,—
To momentary peace it bound
   Our mortal nature's strife;
And still I felt the centre of
   The magic circle there
Was one fair form that filled with love
   The lifeless atmosphere.

v

We paused beside the pools that lie
   Under the forest bough,—
Each seemed as 'twere a little sky
   Gulfed in a world below;
A firmament of purple light
   Which in the dark earth lay,
More boundless than the depth of night,
   And purer than the day—
In which the lovely forests grew,
   As in the upper air,
More perfect both in shape and hue
   Than any spreading there.
There lay the glade and neighbouring lawn,
   And through the dark green wood
The white sun twinkling like the dawn
   Out of a speckled cloud.
Sweet views which in our world above
   Can never well be seen,
Were imagined by the water's love

Of that fair forest green.
And all was interfused beneath
  With an Elysian glow,
An atmosphere without a breath,
  A softer day below.
Like one beloved the scene had lent
  To the dark water's breast,
Its every leaf and lineament
  With more than truth expressed;
Until an envious wind crept by,
  Like an unwelcome thought,
Which from the mind's too faithful eye
  Blots one dear image out.
Though thou art ever fair and kind,
  The forests ever green,
Less oft is peace in Shelley's mind,
  Than calm in waters, seen.

With a Guitar, to Jane

Ariel to Miranda:—Take
This slave of Music, for the sake
Of him who is the slave of thee,
And teach it all the harmony
In which thou canst, and only thou,
Make the delighted spirit glow,
Till joy denies itself again,
And, too intense, is turned to pain;
For by permission and command
Of thine own Prince Ferdinand,
Poor Ariel sends this silent token
Of more than ever can be spoken;
Your guardian spirit, Ariel who,

From life to life, must still pursue
Your happiness;—for thus alone
Can Ariel ever find his own.
From Prospero's enchanted cell,
As the mighty verses tell,
To the throne of Naples, he
Lit you o'er the trackless sea,
Flitting on, your prow before,
Like a living meteor.
When you die, the silent Moon,
In her interlunar swoon,
Is not sadder in her cell
Than deserted Ariel.
When you live again on earth,
Like an unseen star of birth,
Ariel guides you o'er the sea
Of life from your nativity.
Many changes have been run
Since Ferdinand and you begun
Your course of love, and Ariel still
Has tracked your steps, and served your will;
Now, in humbler, happier lot,
This is all remembered not;
And now, alas! the poor sprite is
Imprisoned, for some fault of his,
In a body like a grave;—
From you he only dares to crave,
For his service and his sorrow,
A smile to-day, a song to-morrow.
The artist who this idol wrought,
To echo all harmonious thought,
Felled a tree, while on the steep
The woods were in their winter sleep,
Rocked in that repose divine
On the wind-swept Apennine;

And dreaming, some of Autumn past,
And some of Spring approaching fast,
And some of April buds and showers,
And some of songs in July bowers,
And all of love; and so this tree,—
O that such our death may be!—
Died in sleep, and felt no pain,
To live in happier form again:
From which, beneath Heaven's fairest star,
The artist wrought this loved Guitar,
And taught it justly to reply,
To all who question skilfully,
In language gentle as thine own;
Whispering in enamoured tone
Sweet oracles of woods and dells,
And summer winds in sylvan cells;
For it had learned all harmonies
Of the plains and of the skies,
Of the forests and the mountains,
And the many-voicèd fountains;
The clearest echoes of the hills,
The sofest notes of falling rills,
The melodies of birds and bees,
The murmuring of summer seas,
And pattering rain, and breathing dew,
And airs of evening; and it knew
That seldom-heard mysterious sound,
Which, driven on its diurnal round,
As it floats through boundless day,
Our world enkindles on its way.—
And this it knows, but will not tell
To those who cannot question well
The Spirit that inhabits it;
It talks according to the wit
Of its companions; and no more

Is heard than has been felt before,
By those who tempt it to betray
These secrets of an elder day:
But, sweetly as its answers will
Flatter hands of perfect skill,
It keeps its highest, holiest tone
For our belovèd Jane alone.

To Jane: 'The keen stars were twinkling'

I

The keen stars were twinkling,
And the fair moon was rising among them,
    Dear Jane!
  The guitar was tinkling,
But the notes were not sweet till you sung them
    Again.

II

As the moon's soft splendour
O'er the faint cold starlight of Heaven
    Is thrown,
  So your voice most tender
To the strings without soil had then given
    Its own.

III

The stars will awaken,
Though the moon sleep a full hour later,
    To-night;
  No leaf will be shaken
Whilst the dews of your melody scatter
    Delight.

IV

Though the sound overpowers,
  Sing again, with your dear voice revealing
    A tone
  Of some world far from ours,
Where music and moonlight and feeling
    Are one.

To Edward Williams

I

The serpent is shut out from Paradise.
  The wounded deer must seek the herb no more
    In which its heart-cure lies:
  The widowed dove must cease to haunt a bower
Like that from which its mate with feignèd sighs
    Fled in the April hour.
  I too must seldom seek again
Near happy friends a mitigated pain.

II

Of hatred I am proud,—with scorn content;
  Indifference, that once hurt me, now is grown
    Itself indifferent;
  But, not to speak of love, pity alone
Can break a spirit already more than bent.
    The miserable one
  Turns the mind's poison into food,—
Its medicine is tears,—its evil good.

III

Therefore, if now I see you seldomer,
  Dear friends, dear *friend*! know that I only fly
    Your looks, because they stir

Griefs that should sleep, and hopes that cannot die:
The very comfort that they minister
    I scarce can bear, yet I,
    So deeply is the arrow gone,
Should quickly perish if it were withdrawn.

IV

When I return to my cold home, you ask
    Why I am not as I have ever been.
        You spoil me for the task
    Of acting a forced part in life's dull scene,—
Of wearing on my brow the idle mask
        Of author, great or mean,
    In the world's carnival. I sought
Peace thus, and but in you I found it not.

V

Full half an hour, to-day, I tried my lot
    With various flowers, and every one still said,
        'She loves me—loves me not.'
    And if this meant a vision long since fled—
If it meant fortune, fame, or peace of thought—
        If it meant,—but I dread
    To speak what you may know too well:
Still there was truth in the sad oracle.

VI

The crane o'er seas and forests seeks her home;
    No bird so wild but has its quiet nest,
        When it no more would roam;
    The sleepless billows on the ocean's breast
Break like a bursting heart, and die in foam,
        And thus at length find rest:
    Doubtless there is a place of peace
Where *my* weak heart and all its throbs will cease.

I asked her, yesterday, if she believed
    That I had resolution. One who *had*
      Would ne'er have thus relieved
    His heart with words,—but what his judgement
        bade
Would do, and leave the scorner unrelieved.
      These verses are too sad
    To send to you, but that I know,
Happy yourself, you feel another's woe.

Fragment: Rain

  The fitful alternations of the rain,
  When the chill wind, languid as with pain
  Of its own heavy moisture, here and there
  Drives through the gray and beamless atmosphere.

FROM *Epipsychidion*

I never was attached to that great sect,
Whose doctrine is, that each one should select
Out of the crowd a mistress or a friend,
And all the rest, though fair and wise, command
To cold oblivion, though it is in the code
Of modern morals, and the beaten road
Which those poor slaves with weary footsteps tread,
Who travel to their home among the dead
By the broad highway of the world, and so
With one chained friend, perhaps a jealous foe,
The dreariest and the longest journey go.

True Love in this differs from gold and clay,
That to divide is not to take away.
Love is like understanding, that grows bright,
Gazing on many truths; 'tis like thy light,
Imagination! which from earth and sky,
And from the depths of human fantasy,
As from a thousand prisms and mirrors, fills
The Universe with glorious beams, and kills
Error, the worm, with many a sun-like arrow
Of its reverberated lightning. Narrow
The heart that loves, the brain that contemplates,
The life that wears, the spirit that creates
One object, and one form, and builds thereby
A sepulchre for its eternity.

Mind from its object differs most in this:
Evil from good; misery from happiness;
The baser from the nobler; the impure
And frail, from what is clear and must endure.
If you divide suffering and dross, you may
Diminish till it is consumed away;
If you divide pleasure and love and thought,
Each part exceeds the whole; and we know not
How much, while any yet remains unshared,
Of pleasure may be gained, of sorrow spared:
This truth is that deep well, whence sages draw
The unenvied light of hope; the eternal law
By which those live, to whom this world of life
Is as a garden ravaged, and whose strife
Tills for the promise of a later birth
The wilderness of this Elysian earth.

You are now
In London, that great sea, whose ebb and flow
At once is deaf and loud, and on the shore
Vomits its wrecks, and still howls on for more.
Yet in its depth what treasures! You will see
That which was Godwin,—greater none than he
Though fallen—and fallen on evil times—to stand
Among the spirits of our age and land,
Before the dread tribunal of *to come*
The foremost,—while Rebuke cowers pale and dumb.
You will see Coleridge—he who sits obscure
In the exceeding lustre and the pure
Intense irradiation of a mind,
Which, with its own internal lightning blind,
Flags wearily through darkness and despair—
A cloud-encircled meteor of the air,
A hooded eagle among blinking owls.—
You will see Hunt—one of those happy souls
Which are the salt of the earth, and without whom
This world would smell like what it is—a tomb;
Who is, what others seem; his room no doubt
Is still adorned with many a cast from Shout,
With graceful flowers tastefully placed about;
And coronals of bay from ribbons hung,
And brighter wreaths in neat disorder flung;
The gifts of the most learned among some dozens
Of female friends, sisters-in-law, and cousins.
And there is he with his eternal puns,
Which beat the dullest brain for smiles, like duns
Thundering for money at a poet's door;
Alas! it is no use to say, 'I'm poor!'
Or oft in graver mood, when he will look
Things wiser than were ever read in book,

Except in Shakespeare's wisest tenderness.—
You will see Hogg,—and I cannot express
His virtues,—though I know that they are great,
Because he locks, then barricades the gate
Within which they inhabit;—of his wit
And wisdom, you'll cry out when you are bit.
He is a pearl within an oyster shell,
One of the richest of the deep;—and there
Is English Peacock, with his mountain Fair,
Turned into a Flamingo;—that shy bird
That gleams i' the Indian air—have you not heard
When a man marries, dies, or turns Hindoo,
His best friends hear no more of him?—but you
Will see him, and will like him too, I hope,
With the milk-white Snowdonian Antelope
Matched with his cameleopard—his fine wit
Makes such a wound, the knife is lost in it;
A strain too learnèd for a shallow age,
Too wise for selfish bigots; let his page,
Which charms the chosen spirits of the time,
Fold itself up for the serener clime—
Of years to come, and finds its recompense
In that just expectation.—Wit and sense,
Virtue and human knowledge; all that might
Make this dull world a business of delight,
Are all combined in Horace Smith.—And these,
With some exceptions, which I need not tease
Your patience by descanting on,—are all
You and I know in London.

                              I recall
My thoughts, and bid you look upon the night.
As water does a sponge, so the moonlight
Fills the void, hollow, universal air—
What see you?—unpavilioned Heaven is fair,
Whether the moon, into her chamber gone,

Leaves midnight to the golden stars, or wan
Climbs with diminished beams the azure steep;
Or whether clouds sail o'er the inverse deep,
Piloted by the many-wandering blast,
And the rare stars rush through them dim and fast:—
All this is beautiful in every land.—
But what see you beside?—a shabby stand
Of Hackney coaches—a brick house or wall
Fencing some lonely court, white with the scrawl
Of our unhappy politics;—or worse—
A wretched woman reeling by, whose curse
Mixed with the watchman's, partner of her trade,
You must accept in place of serenade—
Or yellow-haired Pollonia murmuring
To Henry, some unutterable thing.
I see a chaos of green leaves and fruit
Built round dark caverns, even to the root
Of the living stems that feed them—in whose bowers
There sleep in their dark dew the folded flowers;
Beyond, the surface of the unsickled corn
Trembles not in the slumbering air, and borne
In circles quaint, and ever-changing dance,
Like winged stars the fire-flies flash and glance,
Pale in the open moonshine, but each one
Under the dark trees seems a little sun,
A meteor tamed; a fixed star gone astray
From the silver regions of the milky way;—
Afar the Contadino's song is heard,
Rude, but made sweet by distance—and a bird
Which cannot be the Nightingale, and yet
I know none else that sings so sweet as it
At this late hour;—and then all is still—
Now—Italy or London, which you will!

Next winter you must pass with me; I'll have

My house by that time turned into a grave
Of dead despondence and low-thoughted care,
And all the dreams which our tormentors are;
Oh! that Hunt, Hogg, Peacock, and Smith were there,
With everything belonging to them fair!—
We will have books, Spanish, Italian, Greek;
And ask one week to make another week
As like his father, as I'm unlike mine,
Which is not his fault, as you may divine.
Though we eat little flesh and drink no wine,
Yet let's be merry: we'll have tea and toast;
Custards for supper, and an endless host
Of syllabubs and jellies and mince-pies,
And other such lady-like luxuries,—
Feasting on which we will philosophize!
And we'll have fires out of the Grand Duke's wood,
To thaw the six weeks' winter in our blood.
And then we'll talk;—what shall we talk about?
Oh! there are themes enough for many a bout
Of thought-entangled descant;—as to nerves—
With cones and parallelograms and curves
I've sworn to strangle them if once they dare
To bother me—when you are with me there.
And they shall never more sip laudanum,
From Helicon or Himeros;—well, come,
And in despite of God and of the devil,
We'll make our friendly philosophic revel
Outlast the leafless time; till buds and flowers
Warn the obscure inevitable hours,
Sweet meeting by sad parting to renew;—
'To-morrow to fresh woods and pastures new.'

FROM *Julian and Maddalo*

The following morn was rainy, cold and dim:
Ere Maddalo arose, I called on him,
And whilst I waited with his child I played;
A lovelier toy sweet Nature never made,
A serious, subtle, wild, yet gentle being,
Graceful without design and unforeseeing,
With eyes—Oh speak not of her eyes!—which seem
Twin mirrors of Italian Heaven, yet gleam
With such deep meaning, as we never see
But in the human countenance: with me
She was a special favourite: I had nursed
Her fine and feeble limbs when she came first
To this bleak world; and she yet seemed to know
On second sight her ancient playfellow,
Less changed than she was by six months or so;
For after her first shyness was worn out
We sate there, rolling billiard balls about,
When the Count entered.

To William Shelley

Thy little footsteps on the sands
    Of a remote and lonely shore;
The twinkling of thine infant hands,
    Where now the worm will feed no more;
Thy mingled look of love and glee
When we returned to gaze on thee—

Stanzas

I

The sun is warm, the sky is clear,
   The waves are dancing fast and bright,
Blue isles and snowy mountains wear
   The purple noon's transparent might,
   The breath of the moist earth is light,
Around its unexpanded buds;
   Like many a voice of one delight,
The winds, the birds, the ocean floods,
The City's voice itself, is soft like Solitude's.

II

I see the Deep's untrampled floor
   With green and purple seaweeds strown;
I see the waves upon the shore,
   Like light dissolved in star-showers, thrown:
   I sit upon the sands alone,—
The lightning of the noontide ocean
   Is flashing round me, and a tone
Arises from its measured motion,
How sweet! did any heart now share in my emotion.

III

Alas! I have nor hope nor health,
   Nor peace within nor calm around,
Nor that content surpassing wealth
   The sage in meditation found,
   And walked with inward glory crowned—
Nor fame, nor power, nor love, nor leisure.
   Others I see whom these surround—
Smiling they live, and call life pleasure;—
To me that cup has been dealt in another measure.

Yet now despair itself is mild,
   Even as the winds and waters are;
I could lie down like a tired child,
   And weep away the life of care
   Which I have borne and yet must bear,
Till death like sleep might steal on me,
   And I might feel in the warm air
My cheek grow cold, and hear the sea
Breathe o'er my dying brain its last monotony.

V

Some might lament that I were cold,
   As I, when this sweet day is gone,
Which my lost heart, too soon grown old,
   Insults with this untimely moan;
   They might lament—for I am one
Whom men love not,—and yet regret,
   Unlike this day, which, when the sun
   Shall on its stainless glory set,
Will linger, though enjoyed, like joy in memory yet.

Fragment of the Elegy on the Death of Adonis

FROM THE GREEK OF BION

I mourn Adonis dead—loveliest Adonis—
Dead, dead Adonis—and the Loves lament.
Sleep no more, Venus, wrapped in purple woof—
Wake violet-stolèd queen, and weave the crown
Of Death,—'tis Misery calls,—for he is dead.

The lovely one lies wounded in the mountains,
His white thigh struck with the white tooth; he scarce
Yet breathes; and Venus hangs in agony there.
The dark blood wanders o'er his snowy limbs,
His eyes beneath their lids are lustreless,
The rose has fled from his wan lips, and there
That kiss is dead, which Venus gathers yet.

A deep, deep wound Adonis . . .
A deeper Venus bears upon her heart.
See, his belovèd dogs are gathering round—
The Oread nymphs are weeping—Aphrodite
With hair unbound is wandering through the woods,
'Wildered, ungirt, unsandalled—the thorns pierce
Her hastening feet and drink her sacred blood.

Bitterly screaming out, she is driven on
Through the long vales; and her Assyrian boy,
Her love, her husband, calls—the purple blood
From his struck thigh stains her white navel now,
Her bosom, and her neck before like snow.

Alas for Cytherea—the Loves mourn—
The lovely, the beloved is gone!—and now
Her sacred beauty banishes away.
For Venus whilst Adonis lived was fair—
Alas! her loveliness is dead with him.
The oaks and mountains cry, Ai! ai! Adonis!
The springs their waters change to tears and weep—
The flowers are withered up with grief . . .

Ai! ai!   Adonis is dead
Echo resounds   Adonis dead.
Who will weep not thy dreadful woe, O Venus?
Soon as she saw and knew the mortal wound

Of her Adonis—saw the life-blood flow
From his fair thigh, now wasting,—wailing loud
She clasped him, and cried   'Stay, Adonis!
Stay, dearest one, . . .

             and mix my lips with thine—
Wake yet a while, Adonis—oh, but once,
That I may kiss thee now for the last time—
But for as long as one short kiss may live—
Oh, let thy breath flow from thy dying soul
Even to my mouth and heart, that I may suck
That . . .'

Arethusa

I

  Arethusa arose
  From her couch of snows
In the Acroceraunian mountains,—
  From cloud and from crag,
  With many a jag,
Shepherding her bright fountains.
  She leapt down the rocks,
  With her rainbow locks
Streaming among the streams;—
  Her steps paved with green
  The downward ravine
Which slopes to the western gleams;
  And gliding and springing
  She went, ever singing,
In murmurs as soft as sleep;
  The Earth seemed to love her,
  And Heaven smiled above her,
As she lingered towards the deep.

II

Then Alpheus bold,
On his glacier cold,
With his trident the mountains strook;
   And opened a chasm
   In the rocks—with the spasm
All Erymanthus shook.
   And the black south wind
   It unsealed behind
The urns of the silent snow,
   And earthquake and thunder
   Did rend in sunder
The bars of the springs below.
   And the beard and the hair
   Of the River-god were
Seen through the torrent's sweep,
   As he followed the light
   Of the fleet nymph's flight
To the brink of the Dorian deep.

III

'Oh, save me! Oh, guide me!
   And bid the deep hide me,
For he grasps me now by the hair!'
   The loud Ocean heard,
   To its blue depth stirred,
And divided at her prayer;
   And under the water
   The Earth's white daughter
Fled like a sunny beam;
   Behind her descended
   Her billows, unblended
With the brackish Dorian stream:—
   Like a gloomy stain
   On the emerald main

Alpheus rushed behind,—
  As an eagle pursuing
  A dove to its ruin
Down the streams of the cloudy wind.

IV

  Under the bowers
  Where the Ocean Powers
Sit on their pearlèd thrones;
  Through the coral woods
  Of the weltering floods,
Over heaps of unvalued stones;
  Through the dim beams
  Which amid the streams
Weave a network of coloured light;
  And under the caves,
  Where the shadowy waves
Are as green as the forest's night:—
  Outspeeding the shark,
  And the sword-fish dark,
Under the Ocean's foam,
  And up through the rifts
  Of the mountain clifts
They passed to their Dorian home.

V

  And now from their fountains
  In Enna's mountains,
Down one vale where the morning basks,
  Like friends once parted
  Grown single-hearted,
They ply their watery tasks.
  At sunrise they leap
  From their cradles steep
In the cave of the shelving hill;

[83]

At noontide they flow
   Through the woods below
And the meadows of asphodel;
   And at night they sleep
   In the rocking deep
Beneath the Ortygian shore;—
   Like spirits that lie
   In the azure sky
When they love but live no more.

Hymn of Pan

I

From the forests and highlands
   We come, we come;
From the river-girt islands,
   Where loud waves are dumb
     Listening to my sweet pipings.
The wind in the reeds and the rushes,
   The bees on the bells of thyme,
The birds on the myrtle bushes,
   The cicale above in the lime,
And the lizards below in the grass,
Were as silent as ever old Tmolus was,
     Listening to my sweet pipings.

II

Liquid Peneus was flowing,
   And all dark Temple lay
In Pelion's shadow, outgrowing
   The light of the dying day,
     Speeded by my sweet pipings.
The Sileni, and Sylvans, and Fauns,

And the Nymphs of the woods and the waves,
To the edge of the moist river-lawns,
    And the brink of the dewy caves,
And all that did then attend and follow,
Were silent with love, as you know, Apollo,
        With envy of my sweet pipings.

III

I sang of the dancing stars,
    I sang of the daedal Earth,
And of Heaven—and the giant wars,
    And Love, and Death, and Birth,—
        And then I changed my pipings,—
Singing how down the vale of Maenalus
    I pursued a maiden and clasped a reed.
Gods and men, we are all deluded thus!
    It breaks in our bosom and then we bleed:
All wept, as I think both ye now would,
If envy or age had not frozen your blood,
        At the sorrow of my sweet pipings.

The Waning Moon

And like a dying lady, lean and pale,
Who totters forth, wrapped in a gauzy veil,
Out of her chamber, led by the insane
And feeble wanderings of her fading brain,
The moon arose up in the murky East,
A white and shapeless mass—

To the Moon

I

Art thou pale for weariness
Of climbing heaven and gazing on the earth,
  Wandering companionless
Among the stars that have a different birth,—
And ever changing, like a joyless eye
That finds no object worth its constancy?

II

  Thou chosen sister of the Spirit,
That gazes on thee till in thee it pities . . .

A Lament

I

O world! O life! O time!
On whose last steps I climb,
  Trembling at that where I had stood before;
When will return the glory of your prime?
    No more—Oh, never more!

II

Out of the day and night
A joy has taken flight;
  Fresh spring, and summer, and winter hoar,
Move my faint heart with grief, but with delight
    No more—Oh, never more!

On Fanny Godwin

Her voice did quiver as we parted,
    Yet knew I not that heart was broken
From which it came, and I departed
    Heeding not the words then spoken.
        Misery—O Misery,
        This world is all too wide for thee.

FROM *The Triumph of Life: Rousseau*

Struck to the heart by this sad pageantry,
Half to myself I said—'And what is this?
Whose shape is that within the car? And why—'

I would have added—'is all here amiss?—'
But a voice answered—'Life!'—I turned, and knew
(O Heaven, have mercy on such wretchedness!)

That what I thought was an old root which grew
To strange distortion out of the hill side,
Was indeed one of those deluded crew,

And that the grass, which methought hung so wide
And white, was but his thin discoloured hair,
And that the holes he vainly sought to hide,

Were or had been eyes:—'If thou canst, forbear
To join the dance, which I had well forborne!'
Said the grim Feature (of my thought aware).

'I will unfold that which to this deep scorn

Led me and my companions, and relate
The progress of the pageant since the morn;

'If thirst of knowledge shall not then abate,
Follow it thou even to the night, but I
Am weary.'—Then like one who with the weight

Of his own words is staggered, wearily
He paused; and ere he could resume, I cried:
'First, who art thou?'—'Before thy memory,

'I feared, loved, hated, suffered, did and died,
And if the spark with which Heaven lit my spirit
Had been with purer nutriment supplied,

'Corruption would not now thus much inherit
Of what was once Rousseau,—nor this disguise
Stain that which ought to have disdained to wear it;

'If I have been extinguished, yet there rise
A thousand beacons from the spark I bore'—
'And who are those chained to the car?'—'The wise,

'The great, the unforgotten,—they who wore
Mitres and helms and crowns, or wreaths of light,
Signs of thought's empire over thought—their lore

'Taught them not this, to know themselves; their might
Could not repress the mystery within,
And for the morn of truth they feigned, deep night

'Caught them ere evening.'—'Who is he with chin
Upon his breast, and hands crossed on his chain?'—
'The child of a fierce hour: he sought to win

'The world, and lost all that it did contain
Of greatness, in its hope destroyed; and more
Of fame and peace than virtue's self can gain

'Without the opportunity which bore
Him on its eagle pinions to the peak
From which a thousand climbers have before

'Fallen, as Napoleon fell.'—I felt my cheek
Alter, to see the shadows pass away,
Whose grasp had left the giant world so weak

That every pigmy kicked it as it lay;
And much I grieved to think how power and will
In opposition rule our mortal day,

And why God made irreconcilable
Good and the means of good; and for despair
I half disdained mine eyes' desire to fill

With the spent vision of the times that were
And scarce have ceased to be.—'Dost thou behold,'
Said my guide, 'those spoilers spoiled, Voltaire,

'Frederick, and Paul, Catherine, and Leopold,
And hoary anarchs, demagogues, and sage—
      names which the world thinks always old,

'For in the battle Life and they did wage,
She remained conqueror. I was overcome
By my own heart alone, which neither age,

'Nor tears, nor infamy, nor now the tomb
Could temper to its object.'

Index of First Lines